The Night is a Thousand Thoughts

Also by Doug Gregory and published by Ginninderra Press
A Long Way from Essex

Doug Gregory
The Night is a Thousand Thoughts
New & Selected Poems

The Night is a Thousand Thoughts: New & Selected Poems
ISBN 978 1 76109 135 3
Copyright © text Doug Gregory 2021
Cover photo: Fleurieu Moonrise by Doug Gregory

First published 2021 by
GINNINDERRA PRESS
PO Box 3461 Port Adelaide 5015
www.ginninderrapress.com.au

Contents

New Poems
- No Sleep Blues — 11
- The Interview — 13
- All the Retired Old Boys — 14
- Just Be What You Are — 16
- The Office, 1983 — 18
- Poor Old Rodriguez — 20
- Online, 2019 — 22
- Parting Shot — 23
- The Night Has a Thousand Thoughts — 25
- Breaking Point — 28
- Facebook — 29
- Corellas — 30
- How Do We Say 'No' — 32
- I Cling — 34
- Man of the World — 35
- For All That I Have — 37
- Baby Come Back — 38
- Woke Up Dead — 40
- Flesh, Fire and Folly — 42
- Bushfire — 44
- Bully Boys — 45
- Couples — 46
- My Gift Is My Poem — 47
- Now What? — 49
- Cruelty — 50
- Easter — 51
- A Soft Touch — 52
- John and Yoko and 1969 — 53
- Dream Shadow — 54

Rekindled	55
In Excess	57
Sebastian Returns	60
Sweet and Bitter the Day	62
Michelle	63
Indigestion	65
My Dog	66
I Used To Be a Jockey	69
The Big Man	72
Stuffed	74
The Good the Bad and the Ugly	75
Sorry, I Forgot	77
Love Her Madly	79
Facetime	80
Escaping Reality	81
Going Back	82
Keeping Secrets	83
Other Side of the Fence	85
A Pop Star and Two Politicians	86
The Virus 2020	88

From Bindies Only Tickle, 1999

Repetition	91
Back Home	92
Herbal Remedies	93
Seagulls	94
Diluted	95
Separation	96

From A Candle For Tomorrow, 2005

The Sceptic	99
Dinner For Two	100
Looking Back	101

You're Coming Home	102
Horses of War	103

From Where Are the Angels, 2015

Celeste	107
One Word	108
Not So Tough	109
Devastated	111
Looking For Exits	112
Lost For Words	113
A Mystery (The Sentimental Bloke)	114
Contrasting Views	117
Gardening	119
On the Grass	120
Prime Cuts	121
The Priest Hood	122

From Night Café & other poems, 2016

Everything Becomes Nothing	125
Forgiven	127
In My Dreams	129
Coincidence	130
Funeral Atrocity	131
Record Collection	133
Remembering Grandad	136
You Make Loving Fun	140

From A Long Way From Essex, 2019

Seven Shades of Grey	145
Coffee Card	146
If Not For You	148
Now He's Gone	150
Alone Again Or	152
Averages	154

A Day After Dying	157
Baiting and Waiting	158
The Lonely Sun	159

New Poems

No Sleep Blues

My wife says I have hypochondria.
I say I just have insomnia
A newly acquired condition
I have to come to terms with.
Lots of my old-folk buddies speak of this
And how they cope.
Most go for sleeping tablets
But me, being an old new age man
I seek out alternatives.
I ensure there's no light coming through the curtains
So as to not wake me early.
I lightly spray the bedroom
With a lightly scented lavender aroma.
The bottle says it induces sleep.
Then, during a doctor visit, it was suggested
My rhythms are out of sync and he prescribed
Circadin prolonged-release tablets.
Take a couple of weeks to kick in
Though don't seem to have kicked in after three.
Discarding them, another health professional informed me that
An antihistamine pill
Was found to make one drowsy
And advises me to give it a go.
Sometimes it works
Because I believe it.
Sometimes it doesn't
Because I'm sceptical.
I try the magnesium sleep formula
Course of pills two per night times thirty.
No effect.

My body's tired of all this intervention and
One night I just crash out.
Halfway through I'm woken
By a mosquito buzzing in my face.
I don't kill anything but
In a contained rage
Chase the little bastard around the bedroom
Swatting furiously with my bedtime reading paperback.

Now, after closing the curtains
Spraying the lavender
Taking whatever is my latest find in sleep aid alternative medication
I creep around the bedroom
With a small can of insect killer
Looking to put any uninvited guest
To rest.

The Interview

The minister was asked ten questions.
The first
He didn't want to answer
Skirting around the issue.
The second he contradicted what
The opposition minister said yesterday.
One of them…is a blatant liar.
The third he answered
With a torrent of programmed
Well rehearsed standard lines and clichés
Which meant nothing.
The fourth…he sounded ridiculous
Out of touch and condescending.
The next and the next and the next
He combined all his expertise at evasion and trickery
And contempt for the people
Who put him in his job.
The remainder are a blur
As I fought to contain my fury at
Our parliamentarians
Keeping the truth
To themselves.

All the Retired Old Boys

In a corner of South Australia
Are a lot of retirees.
There's not much diversity here
It's mainstream small country town living, cliquish, and
Takes 20 or more years of residing here
To be considered a local, and even then…

It's a big deal being a local.
I've tried, in vain, to appear like a local…a regular sort of guy
But it's hard to sustain.
In the end you have to be yourself, don't you
And I'm glad to not look too different
Like black or Asian or something.
I can do without that sort of isolation.

But, back to the retirees
In particular the old boys
Lots of them
Wandering around with their little dogs
Sitting aimlessly in the pubs
Thinking alone in reflection.

Aside from those in the men's shed
Or the administrators of local sports teams
I'm acquainted with several of them
Old Reg and Mick and Will, Mike and Max and Phil
And many more.
Jack, he takes to daytime naps
To escape the bane of tedium

Lenny's on a desperate search
To find himself a new woman.
Vic goes around in a state of resignation
Forever whingeing that there's nothing to do
But nothing you can do about it.
Barry laments the passing of the old days and the old ways
When men were men and women knew their place.
Colin argues incessantly with his wife
Constantly making the point that retirement is no life.
Davy's become reclusive
Locks himself away
Just watches TV all night and day.
Martin is infuriating
Believing he's discovered all new wisdom.
He likes to join you for conversation
But when you talk he never listens
And when he does, he doesn't hear.
Then Ray, trying to preserve long-departed youth
Extra lotion on his face and lengthening thinning hair in a ponytail.
They are the retired old boys.

Me, I just get the blues about being old
But then again,
I got the blues a lot when I was young.

Just Be What You Are

The centrepiece of my day was
A trip to the barber
Or, more correctly, the hairdresser.
Greatly anticipating this, with thoughts of
A new image, look younger, more healthy
More 'with it'
I commence my journey.
A very young hairdresser
'What would you like?' he asks
Thinking momentarily and glancing around
I direct his attention to a picture on the wall
Of George Clooney.
The hairdresser, I detected, looked bemused
And tried to disguise it.
'So you want it a bit shorter?'
I think, I can't go too much shorter.
Just a little shorter, thank you.
He starts clipping away.
After several minutes I observe that I'm not yet
Looking like George Clooney.
His face is fuller
His hair is thicker and darker
And grows from the front of his forehead.
His eyes are clear, he has no lines on his face
And the top of his head is flat
Mine is pointy.

The hairdresser clips on and
I'm looking less like George Clooney with every passing second.
As he carefully starts trimming
What was once, in another age, my Beatles fringe
It is severely revealing
An extremely receding hairline
And I'm beginning to look like a monk.

So, unless
I fill out my face with botox
Put make-up under my eyes
And go buy myself a wig
This little fantasy-induced ambition
Is doomed to fail.

I leave the hairdresser, return home
And ponder my next
Image-changing enterprise.

The Office, 1983

No computers yet, but
A delivery of
New modern electronic typewriters
Was met with amazement and wow
By the ladies in the typing pool.
How will we ever master them?
It was the early stage
Of the modern age
But old ways were rife.
The boss was often a grovelling, joking, groping
Unattractive small man.
A time of jobs for the boys.
Gender superiority and harassment
Were commonplace with
Frequent sleazy comments about
One's figure and clothing and
Touchy, feely strokes of the arms and bottom.
Bullying was on a grand scale
Sometimes savage, sometimes subtle.
Occ. health and safety practices were
Virtually non-existent
And one had to part the air of tobacco smoke
To enter most offices.

With the penalties dished out today
For these offences
Most managers would be broke by fines
Fired
Or spending the rest of their days
In the nick.

A time of innocence…
No, it wasn't.

Poor Old Rodriguez

I'm going back some decades.
There was a girl, Marcia
Not, at first, the most striking of girls
But she grew on me
I couldn't help it…I fell for her.
She was married, to Rodriguez
Though it was of no concern to me.
Rodriguez worked in prisons.
He was, by all accounts
A dumb bastard, insensitive
Loved his football team
And would drag Marcia along
To all three grades
Every weekend of the season.
She promptly left him and we got together
Became a couple of roaming, hippie gypsies
Dope smoking, drinking, hooking up to welfare cash handouts
Being carefree and fairly stupid
Finally living in one room in Kings Cross, Sydney.

It petered out
Though we stayed friends
And Marcia never went back to Rodriguez.

Fast forward ten years
I was introduced to a girl, Melanie
Who was the best friend of a girlfriend of mine.
I fell for her straight away and
She fell for me.
We had an intense affair, lasting about a year.
Seemed, at one point, it would never end.

Melanie worked in prisons.
She would tell me one day about a colleague of hers.
His name was Rod
And Rod had been trying, fruitlessly
To get it on with her.
She told him that she has a man
She told him my name
And a bit of my history.
Rod, whose actual name was Rodriguez
Over time, putting all things together
Was stunned to realise
That it was the same man with whom
A decade earlier
His wife had run off with
And, understandably, was livid.

Now, that, I declare, in a big city
Is a case of
Rotten luck.

Melanie and I…we petered out.

Online, 2019

If somebody had told me
Twenty-five years ago
That there would soon be
A little device invented
That will take the place of:
A telephone
A public telephone box
A camera
A photo processing shop
A newspaper
A newsagent
Stamps, envelopes, pens, pencils and writing pads
Books, bookshops and libraries
Records, record players, transistor radios
Postmen, journalists and weather presenters
Banking offices, tax offices, passport offices, betting shops
Department stores, stationers and pet shops
Replace birthday cards, Christmas cards and postcards
Diaries, notebooks, telephone directories and filing cabinets
And…
Talk to anyone you want, anywhere in the world
At anytime…and look at them while you do it
And…
You can hold it all in one hand
I would have said
'Oh my god!
Will it also replace politicians, churches and councils?'

Parting Shot

Walking down the main street
My dog just ahead of me
I see a guy sitting at a table
Outside the takeaway, next to the butcher's shop.
He too had a dog
And mine approached his and
They communicated – as little friendly dogs do.
The guy remarked, That's a sight
Two dogs hanging together outside the butcher's door
And we both laughed.

It occurred to me that
This chap
With his long dark hair and moustache
About twenty years old (fifty younger than me)
Slim and kind of hippie-looking
Looked about exactly as I did
When I was his age.
So I made the comment
That he reminded me of me
Fifty years ago, and how time goes by so fast.
Again, we laughed and, momentarily
He seemed stumped for words
Briefly eyeing me up and down.
I could almost see him thinking,
I can't imagine that
As I presented a little overweight
Old man-ish with thin grey hair.

And he, not for a second
Being able to comprehend
The certainty and inevitability
Of the passing of fifty years
And what it does to one.

He said something
Not necessarily uncomplimentary
Though implying that he thought it
Hard to believe.

We had a couple more
Short friendly exchanges and
Departing, I touched him on the shoulder and said.
Nice to meet you.
You'll probably look just like me
In fifty years time.

And we both laughed.

The Night Has a Thousand Thoughts

I was nodding off
In front of the TV at 9.30 p.m.
It's now 2.30 a.m., I'm in bed
And haven't slept a wink.
This is the time
A thousand thoughts go through my mind
I call it silly thinking
All the worries and chores
Come to the fore
Everything is amplified and magnified
And rarely anything is resolved.
All the advice
And sensible ideas I've been given, like
Just relax, use your mantra, stop thinking
Seem to desert me.
Loads and loads of thoughts pop up
One after the other overlapping endlessly
Melodic and haunting
Scary and daunting.
Don't know how I can cope with all this…
Why are David and Eileen so mean
Do they really like me at the social club
Something was said…and taken the wrong way
What if I forget my thoughts on
The live radio interview
Will the next packet of smokes be my last.
I've got so much to do
But life goes by so fast
Will I ever get to finish my masterful poem
The one about injustice I want the world to see.

And why did I take the conventional path
When I strived to be the bohemian.
Oh the despair and the torment of this restless night
And there's more, there's more…
Why do I so want to see the people
I once wanted to leave
Why do I dwell on the past so much.
It's gone
And she's not coming back.
How much life have I now got left
Will it end before I finally crack.
My wife's sleeping peacefully
My dog stretched out blissfully
Whilst I'm lying here in a heap.
There's a hissing in my ears and
My heart beats louder
I'm becoming overheated and my mouth fills with powder
So I get up and go for a leak.
Everything seems much less intense
When I'm upright and switch on the light.
But there's more, still more
All the things I can do nothing about…
How could the government have made that atrocious decision
When will my noisy neighbours finally move out
When will they stop dumping shit in the river.
My optimism's fading and I'm full of self-doubt
And the future, what about the future.
Life can be good, and fun at times
But rarely does it end very well.

This is a condition only I can sort out and
I finally say stop, that's enough.
I think of a big blank black night.
Next thing I know…
It's morning
And almost everything seems all right.

Breaking Point

Was thinking about my mother
In the early hours today
As one does when a parent dies
Scanning her whole life
At least that which I'm aware of.

A simple, uneducated London woman
Born with a disability
Whose childhood was spent in the
Gruesome 1930s and 40s
I never really knew her that well.
She had an inner strength that
I didn't appreciate.

Her life seemed to change
For the worse and forever
When the new generation of families
Moved into the district
On the outskirts of the village where she lived.
Their kids were brats and uncontrolled
And one day they came into the village
And slaughtered all the ducks on the pond.

Mum told me this
With tears in her voice
Some years ago
And her early onset dementia
Almost
At once
Became full blown.

Facebook

It's time I tried the Facebook thing.
Everyone I know is doing it.
It's 2019 and
I'm falling behind, further and further.
I do what's required, then
Just hit the button.
I'm in.

I cast my mind back and wonder
Whose name, from my past, whom I haven't had contact with
For, say, 30 or more years
Should I look up.
Then, I remember Trish.
We had a relationship
For a couple of years in the late 70s.
It was good and
I still think of her.

I enter her name, then
Surprise, then
Shock…she's looking right at me!
A photograph, of a recent time.
She's barely changed
Same smile and expression
I can almost feel her.

We were once intimate and now
The whole world is sharing her.

Corellas

Every year, late spring
They arrive
A flock of corellas, about a thousand strong
Screeching in unison as they fly above us
Seeking out a temporary home
In the trees of our town.

They cause much ill feeling
Anger mostly, amongst the townsfolk.
Cull them, shoot them, poison them
JUST DO SOMETHING about them
Are the cries.
It's their kingdom too, I'm thinking
But we, people, have the power.
We determine what lives where, when, how
We determine what lives.

I get a little irritated
When the birds spend a few days
Tearing the nuts off my pine tree
Though only because
I have to clean up after them
And, anyway, it's something to do and I have other bigger issues
To get wound up over
And I don't want to kill them.

When passers-by yell
With passion and energy
'They're a fucking pest, aren't they?'
I nod half-heartedly and
Don't want to discuss it.

I muse as I clean out the gutter and sweep my drive
Why don't you just
Bugger off and vent your passionate anger at
Bankers and priests and
Dishonest politicians
And violent men on the streets and
Corrupt governments
And drug and chemical companies
And mining companies
And other polluters
Despicable radio talkback hosts
And all the other scum of your own species
And leave the corellas
To live in harmony.

How Do We Say 'No'

Been trying to figure out
How to tell someone
Who keeps on saying
We've got to get you over soon
To our place
For dinner
That we don't want to go to your place
Soon, or for dinner.
How do we say no
Without hurting their feelings.
It's not that they're the problem
We're the problem
Because we don't want to go.
They're simple people
They are kind
But they're not our kind
They're in our face, creep into our space.
They are
When all is said and done
Just another couple acquaintance
Of which we've made hundreds
And, despite knowing
That everyone is unique
They are remarkably similar
To most other couples
Not much better, not much worse
Whose place we would not seek to visit
To have dinner at, or
Spend countless precious hours in their company
Extending the mostly tiresome conversations
We usually have at the club.

It has become a dread
To avoid.
Will we go to the club tonight?
They may be there
And so we deprive ourselves of
What once used to be
A pleasant short evening out
Sitting alone, the two of us
Couple of drinks
Mini conversations with
Now familiar-looking faces
Everyone seemed friendly, left us alone
Albeit with an open invitation
To join them
If we wanted to.

These days it's
Hello you two
We want you to come over
You must come over
When do you want to come
What day suits you best
We must get you over.

They are just being nice
Though want to know what we're all about.
They are curious.
We don't want to be a curiosity
Just want to be left alone.

Now,
How do we put that into words?

I Cling

It's seven-thirty, just awake
I've been in a dream
A kaleidoscope of
Passion and drama
Excitement and emotion
Bizarre and exotic
Stimulating and erotic.
It was all bits and pieces
People and places
Events and moments
Childhood, adulthood
From the past.
It all came together
As if it was the last day of my life.

Man of the World

Took my first trip to the city today
As an old man
People stepping out of my way
Inviting me to cross ahead, offering their seat.
It mostly looks the same
Feels the same, sounds the same, smells the same
Then, I begin to spot the differences
Scaffolding everywhere, cranes
New regulations.
Adelaide…
A city on the up trying to be like
Any other bigger city.
It's not my town.
I've been a gypsy for my seventy years
A home here, a home there.
I'm not a part of Adelaide
I don't belong, or share its history
I'm a stranger, an outsider, on the fringe.
I keep walking, through the streets
My legs aching, my hair grey and thinning
Amidst the energy and vibrancy
My clothes outdated
I tower over everyone in terms of years survived.
Lots of younger, modern people
A new way of speaking with teeny, weeny voices.
No more record stores.
I dream of vinyl 45s with A-sides and B-sides.
A cup of coffee in a café now has 25 options

A request for tax forms at the tax office is met with
Sorry, can't do…we're all digital here.
As the oldest person around
I feel like a child that
Needs to be taken by the hand
No longer the man of the world I once was.
Thankfully, I meet up with my wife who
Just spent two hours wandering through the wondrous
Art Gallery of SA
Taking in the Impressionists exhibition
A nice, normal, old-fashioned thing to do.

But I had my adventure, bought some clothing and a book
And it's put me on a little high.
Now, we're back to Goolwa
Where the air is sweet, the birds sing you songs and
You can almost touch the sky.

For All That I Have

I stopped in my tracks this morning
Stopped and thought about everything
Took a breather and said a thank you
For all that I have
Some would call it a prayer
But I've never done prayers
I was deep inside
Being deeply grateful
For being what I am having what I have giving what I give
It felt like a living memorial to life
As it is
At this moment
I'm here with my thoughts and feelings
With my eyes my mouth my ears
My legs my arms my lungs my heart
All in good order
Despite feeling a little lack-lustre
I'm here with my wife
Comforting, caring, reassuring
My dog
Who waits patiently
For the early morning attention she demands of me
I'm here with the new dawn
Everything is as it was yesterday
My friends and my things
Are all here today
It won't always be this way
But it's uplifting
To stop and think
That I'm blessed to have
What I have today.

Baby Come Back

When you're living in an ageing body
There are many things
To be wary of.
One reaches a time
With an unpreparedness
When a whole new set of priorities
Come to the fore
And it is no trivial matter.

It arrives gradually
Though in reality is a sudden onset
The first sign of something not right
A visit to the doctors
And it giveth them the opportunity
To inform you
You are now old!
With warnings of
Rising blood pressure
Cancer
Arthritis
Diabetes
Dementia
Et cetera et cetera, and
The necessity for
A modified diet
Reduced drinking
No smoking and
An adjusted lifestyle.

It's not unusual to become
Preoccupied, obsessed
With all this new information
Red lights
Not yet flashing
But they're switched on.
Myself, like the typical 70-year-old
Has begun the process of decaying
Nothing too alarming as yet
And, still thinking like a young man
Taking uncalculated risks and gambles.
My wife, a little older and
With whom I've grown for the past forty years
Naturally faces the same future
So it becomes a double whammy.

Faced with all this unpredictability…
A funny turn, a heart attack, a stroke
When you think of it
It truly is no joke.
She has the added curse of a dicey hip
Causing her on occasion to falter and slip
So when she takes her morning walk
And a couple of hours have passed
I'm thinking of her on that treacherous track
And saying to myself repeatedly, mantra-like
Baby, baby, please come back.

Woke Up Dead

An old friendly acquaintance of mine
Whom I'll call Grumble
For the purpose of this verse and
To preserve his identity
Was the most miserable person
I've ever come across.
Not so old, sixty or so
He deteriorated much more severely
Than the rest of our little social circle.
A good morning, how are you greeting
Was always met with 'I'm jaded.'
He would complain
When it was hot or cold, windy or calm
Sunset or dawn, sober or pissed
Would ensure that his wife
Never had a nice night out
If other women
Were not amenable to his advances
Which they never were.
He would describe himself as
A silly old sod
A grumpy old git
And, if one agreed
Would react in a barely contained emotional fit.

Grumble said to me one day
As we encountered each other in a shopping mall
I suppose we'll just keep doing this
Walking around aimlessly
Going home getting bored
Waking up again with nothing to do
Until we drop dead.

I can't remember what I replied.
It was just Grum being his usual self.

Recently the wretched Grumble
Died in his sleep.
He would have been so happy, I reckon
If only he could have woken up
The next day
To discover he was dead.

Flesh, Fire and Folly

When I was twenty-two or twenty-three
I visited a doctor
Not a common practice for me back then.

I'd left home
Just a couple of years earlier and
Amongst my many newly acquired freedoms were
Staying up late, drinking
Letting my hair grow longer and longer, so I looked like a hippy
Getting involved in a romantic relationship, and
Ceasing visits to doctors and dentists.

However,
In all this new indulgence
I became, as we then termed it,
A bit run-down and in need of a tonic.
I was confused, frequently hungover
And felt I couldn't cope
So I visited a doctor.
I didn't know what to say was wrong with me
I skirted around things
Stumbling and bumbling and mumbling
But the doctor, in his wisdom, and
With his life experience
Figured out what my problems were.
He was an elderly man, a gentleman
His name was Dr J.J. Hamilton.
I didn't really want pills
Or an analyst
Or any kind of medical intervention

He detected this.
He spoke to me in lyrical, understanding, kindly tones
Acknowledging my confused state and acute sensitivity.
I was instantly lifted.
He then gave me a book
A book he had written
Of poetry
Titled *Flesh, Fire and Folly.*
It spoke of love and desire, of secrets and dreams
Of the planet, the universe and other things.
I guess the title is explanatory.

I left his surgery to go home…with the book
And read it over and over.
Although not fully comprehending all the poetic expression
It made me realise that
I wasn't alone
With all my emotional turmoil.

I never saw the doctor again.

To this day
I still have the book
And to this day
That visit
With no prescription
No referral
No follow-up
Was the most rewarding and beneficial doctor's appointment
I've ever had.

Bushfire

It's all gone
Melted into a mass
Or
Burnt to nothing.

Today it's raining.

Raindrops
The only life now here
Blending with the echoes of before
In a dead
Empty space.

It's all gone
Like yesterday.

Bully Boys

Bully boys
All around the world
Are bursting their way to the top
Leading nations with
Arrogance, deceit and insults
With offensive and threatening rhetoric.
No lessons learnt from history there.

While, in our schools
Anti-bullying campaigns
Are taking top priority.
What
Do we expect our kids
To make of it all?

Couples

Through my observations
I think it may be wiser
And likely more successful
To meet a lifetime love
At age sixty – rather than twenty.
It is unfair
To expect one, at sixty
To play and wriggle around in bed
As they did at twenty.
It is unnatural
To live together
For a long period
In rooms
With clocks and air conditioning.
One becomes impatient
As the other stays calm
One becomes overheated while the other
Keeps cool.

We think we're the same
But, over time, grow into differences.

My Gift Is My Poem

I get nervy, edgy, anxious, all that
When people say,
Hi, Doug, coming over your way soon
To catch up and
Stay awhile
Even long-time friends, family, people I love.
But there are exceptions
And they're not family
Or lifelong friends
They are my wife's best friend, Pat
And husband Bob
Pat and Bob from Canberra.
They are easy, natural, non-judgemental
Sincere, sometimes funny, never resentful.
Pat is loud and proud
Upright and direct
Straight through the crash barriers if so required
She is unselfconscious
And once turned heads when announcing
In a pizza restaurant
I really fancy the nine-inch Moroccan.
Bob is softly, with the image of
The retired professor of handymansmith.
They are good old left-leaning fair dinkum Aussies.
My life is always merrier
With Pat and Bob from Canberra.

With milestone occasions approaching
It is difficult, at our vintage
To buy gifts
When they don't need any more 'things'.
My gift
Is my poem
And this one's for you.

Now What?

She said, But I love him
I said, You can't trust him

She said, We go out to dinner, he's generous and we share the cost
I said, He's well off, has a good income but he's mean

She said, He's so kind and considerate and he always listens
I said, He's cruel, he's selfish and is always scheming

She said, But he's caring and strong and healthy
I said, He doesn't care, he's weak and carries
Sexually transmitted diseases

She said, he's so good-looking
I said, Is he, so what

She said, He has all these plans and what we can do together
I said, But you can't trust him

She said what she said
Because she believes it
I said what I said
Because I know it.

What now?

Cruelty

Some of it is just the way it is
Some of it is intended
And some
Is because of thoughtlessness.

Walking around
I hear people being cruel to each other.
Reading the news
Cruelty jumps out from every page.
Driving around
I see a dead dry parched land.
Looking closer
I see little baby lambs and
Little baby calves
With nothing for them
Or their mothers
To eat.
They're lambing and calving
In the middle of a drought!

Easter

For God's sake
The church leaders are calling once more for hope and peace
Which the majority have never listened to and
The Pope is blessing and kissing the feet
Of murderers, rapists and thieves.
Our party political leaders
In the midst of an election campaign
Call a truce and 'a ceasefire' to hostilities
As though we should all ready ourselves for social warfare.
The evangelical and Pentecostal rosy-red-cheeked Hillsong flock
Are at it again in their stadium-sized venues
Waving their arms in unison in a frenzy of excitement
To their disco beat sound-alike religious pop star idols.

It's all been done before
It's all been said before.

For goodness sake
When
Will my fellow humans
Start to behave like good god-fearing folk
And heed all these messages.
With priests and carers
Politicians and leaders
Banks and multinationals
Terrorists and teachers
And a multitude of creeps walking amongst us
One may wonder where the hope and peace is coming from.

A Soft Touch

The curtains are parted enough
To see the beams
Of sunlight
Streaming in

Looking out
It's beautiful, peaceful
It's calm
Another sunny day
Contrasting the cold, harsh world just beyond
With its filth, its cruelty, its sadness
I'm on the brink, at the edge
Recent liaisons have
Tempered my temporary contentment.

I hold close and
Cuddle my dog
She's now
She's warm
She's here.

John and Yoko and 1969

Fifty years ago…
It was the climax to the new world rising
Turning from grey to psychedelic
And turning twenty-one
1969, together
With the love of my life
We breathed the same air as

The Beatles…still making beautiful music
Elvis Presley…who still graced the stage
Bob Dylan and Joan Baez…the voices of our generation
Andy Warhol…causing a stir in the art world
Richard Nixon…causing unrest and division in America
Harold Wilson…smoking his pipe in Westminster
Neil Armstrong…leaving for the moon
Elizabeth Taylor…on her fifth marriage
Bobby Moore…captain of football world champions England
Joplin, Hendrix and Morrison…all legends in their time
Woodstock…the event of the decade
The Maharishi…meditating the world to harmony
Nelson Mandela…serving his time in isolation
Muhammad Ali…fighting against war and hate
And
John and Yoko…walking hand in hand for love and peace.

It all seems so surreal
All seems so dreamlike and far away
It's how it was fifty years ago
It was fifty years ago today.

Dream Shadow

I don't know why, but
You've just spent
The whole night with me.
We were in Sydney, in London
Even Hilldene Avenue in Essex
I don't know why!

You were insignificant when I knew you
Way down the list of desirables
And here you are
Attached to me
Giving me orders
Friendly with all my friends and family
Yet, in real life
You were a menace.

Now, I find myself
Living in your shadow
All day long.

Rekindled

There is little to compare with
The excitement, anticipation
Fulfilment and satisfaction
That one has
From having a solid friend.
Goodness and honesty
Debate and enlightenment
Joyfulness and emotion.
I have one such friend
The
Unknown
Poet
Who has the rare qualities
Of truth, humility, openness and
An extraordinary ability
To understand
The patience to listen and
To capture your attention with his
Wise, all-knowing poetic expression.

A long time ago I had a similar friend
Free-thinking, open-minded, generous of spirit
Who brought me to
A new awareness in life.
He was my guru
I attached to his every utterance.
Estranged for more than twenty years
My next meetings with him were a mystery.
He had seemingly become a
Bitter, bigoted, racist lunatic

Obsessed with the legacy of
Winston Churchill
Jesus Christ
And a hatred of Immigrants and Gays.
Denying and rejecting of all doctors' advice
When addressing his mounting health problems
He seemed to have a death wish.

I've never come to terms with it
Never understood it
Never got over it.

He once stood out
As a mighty man
Amongst the hundreds, thousands
Of people I had ever met
Now he's fallen
Back to the pack.
I've never got over it.

My new friend
Shows no sign
Of such a transformation.

And from the friendship of such a person
My joy
Is rekindled.

In Excess

I'm an obsessive type
And compulsive
Decadent and reckless I'm often reminded.
There are several things I have
An abundance of passion for
Some, and not all are healthy, are
Going out for dinner
With my wife, who adds spice to the night by looking seductive
Eating and drinking
Music and smoking
A moderate gamble in the casino lounge at the pub
Then going home, continuing on
With the wine, tobacco and music
Staying up late
Letting the desire take us
Wherever it takes us.
A comprehensive night out, and in
With no half measures
That extends to the early hours of the following day.

I cannot bring myself
To do any of these things
Independently of each other.
Eating and drinking go together
Drinking goes with smoking
Music and everything go together
The night is not complete
Unless it's all-in
Everything or nothing.

It's not so much self-destructive as
Self-indulgent.
It makes me feel high and happy
Takes away my stresses and anxieties
I stop thinking about the impoverished millions
Slaughterhouses and injustice.
It gives me something to look forward to
Keep on living for
Better than tablets, analysts and being sensible
Whatever gets you through your life.
I was doing this at twenty
And thirty and fifty
And now seventy.
I'm still here, still standing, with no end in sight
Having something to keep on living for.

At seventy I've realised that
I've rarely ever taken notice
Of all the good considerate life-prolonging advice
That people and professionals and experts
Have given me during my lifetime.
Irresponsible, stupid, undisciplined?
Perhaps, but
I always revert to my own formula
For happiness, fulfilment and longevity.
Time will tell.

The only downside is
I have three wasted days
On hangover
Before I return to normal.
Three days times all those occasions, more than I could count
Adds up to a lot of time
But…one can't have everything.

Sebastian Returns

Dear Sebastian, you really are
Such an arsehole
You're at it again
Popping up in my mind, reminding me of
How beauty can turn
To ugly
All the deceit and lies and contempt
Has been revealed
Among others, by our mutual acquaintance
The brat
Whom you know by another name
She's disclosed all
Spilled the beans on you
It came as shock at first
But now there's only numbness
I've never been so slow-cooked
By anyone before.
You once said you're
An Australiaphile
You idiot…there's no such word
Though I understand if you invented it
It confirms you're not a worldly man
In your little box
With all your secretive stuff.
The ghost of who I thought you were persists
In creeping up behind me
From time to time
Blackening my days.

I wonder, if you get to read this
With its fictitious names
That you'll ever recognise yourself.

Sweet and Bitter the Day

I go to the front garden
Pick up my delivered daily newspaper
Check inside the back page and
Discover my horse won the late race
A nice 20 to 1 shot, which gives me a nice little buzz
A good start to the day.
Then, to the back garden
A couple of bird whistles and I await
The response from my ten-year-old pet rescued finch
No reply…I approach his aviary
And discover he's cold and lifeless on the floor beside his food bowl.
The thrill vanishes instantly
And grief takes over.

Now, Seneca, the Roman, of two thousand years ago
Has taught me
To expect the unexpected
To expect anything and everything and in particular
That which one does not welcome
That no one is entitled
To a good and happy and prosperous life
Which is not what I grew up naively believing.
His examples of what we should expect
Of catastrophic accidents, unbearable broken hearts, earthquakes
Dying in grotesque circumstances and so on
Are far more severe than my little matter, nevertheless
Significant in my life.
But this teaching has served me well, in one sense, and
Been inclined to make me rather morbid in another.

Michelle

I've never immortalised you in poetry
Until now…maybe
Will it seem like an open letter to the world or
Something from my heart, only for you?

I've never really known
What was real.
It's more than three decades past
In 1984/85.
Was it my greatest misadventure?
I've never quite known who's to blame
You or me.
I don't know if you broke my heart
Or just simply made me free.
I don't know if I broke your heart.
I was so blinded, carried away
I could hardly see.

The outcome of each encounter was impossible to foretell
Sometimes a furnace, other times an ice bath.
The drink and the future went to our heads
And my best friend warned me to beware.

You had the car
You sped off and
Left me numb, released, hopeful.
I don't know if I loved you
Was in love with you
Or you were the greatest passion.

For years after
I had a shock attack
Each time
I thought I saw you
In a crowd.

I never truly knew
What was real.
And I don't want to think of it any more.

Indigestion

The quaint romantic restaurant

Was a most unfulfilling experience

With their over the top, giggling waiter people

And background music

In the foreground.

The building was beautiful

The human beings dreadful.

My Dog

Some years ago I was asked
If I'd look after
A little white dog for three days.
I said yes.
The owners dropped off
Five-year-old Mary
And I haven't seen them since.
No dramas…we reached an arrangement
Mostly by texting
An easy communication means these days.
They didn't want her
I did.
Mary is beautiful, cute, cuddly
Almost soft toy like
A West Highland terrier (Westy)
The image of the dog on the can of MyDog dog food
Everybody loves her at first sight.
If you're not familiar with the breed
They all look the same:
Little, white, square head.
That, of course, is not true
A bit like the tourist going to Japan
And saying all Japanese look the same.
But, from distance, all Westies look alike
You have to get up close
To spot the differences
And when you get close up
Every one of them will look different and respond different
Just like people.
So the Westy is little, cute and white.

I'm a big chap, exaggerated when standing next to my dog
Very macho, some have said
Though I'm not a macho man
And when I walk around my town
With my little dog
It's commonplace to get hideously juvenile comments
Shouted at me
By the would-be macho men
Things like Get a real dog, mate, and
Is he a killer or what?
To which I reply
He's a girl
And so wind them up a little more.
Probably it wouldn't be an issue
In the more trendy, city places
Norwood, Unley, Burnside and so on
But in my town
I have to conclude
The minds are not so broad.

My dog has taught me much.
Though nearly fourteen years old
Her behaviour is akin to that of a two-year-old child
Cheeky, sneaky, a little brattish at times
Spoilt, so gets her own way often
Also intelligent
Knows how to cure herself
Doesn't worry, gets on with it
And it's a new day.

If her walk or feed or attention
Is not forthcoming when she demands
So be it.
Lots of the stuff I get impatient over.
The trouble is, of course
Unlike a child, in most cases
One outlives one's dog
Then you're left
Broken-hearted.

I Used To Be a Jockey

I was a kid, just left school.
A few days later I was thrust into
My working life.
Easter Sunday, 1964
Escorted to the saddle room
By the imposing, larger than life
Racehorse trainer Mr Watts, I was introduced.
'This is the new apprentice.'
Having had a rather sheltered upbringing
With very little socialising
I was anxious in the midst of all the strangers
All men and boys
All confident and tough
All loud and swearing.
I was overwhelmed, looking around, overawed.
Is there anyone famous here
A champion jockey maybe?
I've never seen anyone famous.
That first encounter shook me to the core.
My dad wanted me to be a jockey.
I can't remember if I did, but
The delicious thought of being one
Being famous
Being rich
Was very powerful
And I was completely unprepared
For the hard times that lay ahead.

I was never cut out to be a jockey
Too fragile of body and mind
But I looked forward
With hope and
The possibility of a miracle.

I was a tall lad
Taller than all the other apprentices
And, as we walked around Newmarket together
I imagined
All the girls would see me as
A new baby-faced fully fledged jockey in town, and therefore
Had a nice ego trip.

I battled away
Riding giant, frisky thoroughbreds before sunrise
Falling off, getting back on
Mucking out stables
Six and a half days a week from 5 a.m.
Often longing to be back home, many miles away
In the easy, safe company of my mum, dad and brothers.

I rode the Heath
With the legends:
Lester Piggott, Scobie Breasley, Doug Smith.
I met and shook hands with
Lords, ladies and American millionaires.
My failings, however, were obvious.
I was always going to be too heavy
Didn't mix too well
Could not bring myself to swear all the time
And got more scared after each fall.
Then, one day
I addressed my boss
The famous Mr Watts
As Jack
His actual name
As appeared in the daily newspapers.
That
Was the end.
He reported it to the head stable man and
I was subjected to the biggest bollocking of my short life.
Who the fuck do you think you are!
I copped a beating…and called it a day.
I never was cut out to be a jockey.

The Big Man

Not easy…making new friends
Reliable, trustworthy, sincere
When you have planted yourself into
A new district at a ripe age of sixty-something.
The big man and I
Befriended one another.
A professional man with
A high standing in the community
He always sees himself as
The biggest person in the room
Not in stature
But in status
In qualifications
In social skills
In popularity
Big in confidence…and ego.
He has a way with words, pithy
A way with getting his own way.
Indeed, a way with getting away with whatever
Any way he decides upon.
He befriends one with ease and assurance
He has power
But, like vast numbers of people with power
He is prone to be corrupt and
Have another side, a b-side
That contrasts greatly with the a-side
As I discovered
With the big man.

He draws you in
Gives his time, assistance, compliments
Then, at a moment of his convenience and choosing
Will spit you out
And play a juvenile game
Of behaving hideously
Upon seeing you in the main street or a café
Half hiding his face
And walking awkwardly, contorted, sideways
Like a spider
To avoid the confrontation.

The specifics and details are not necessary to mention
And I now sit here
In the shadow of all the good deeds of yesteryear
And battle to come to grips
With the betrayal.

Stuffed

Just celebrated my 71st
Lovely peaceful friendly setting
A platter of fine local produce
Enough to feed a neighbourhood.
Now I'm sitting here stuffed and bloated
Trying to digest a large dose of guilt and
Thinking I might pass on dessert.

How can I reconcile this with
A couple of billion people on earth
In a not so friendly environment
Who might eat this much in a month
If they're lucky.

How can I go about and
Enjoy myself thus
When I have this
On my mind?

It's a day to day thing.
Today I indulge
Tomorrow
I attempt to justify it.

The Good the Bad and the Ugly

I've always wondered
Just where I fit in
What 'type' I am
To what group I belong.
I left my home, my family, my country
My wife, my friends
My cat and all my things
Settled in a range of different places and
Moved on
When there was nothing to stay for.

In my time
I've been described as…
A good man
A loving man
A caring man
A learned man
A secretive man
A compassionate man
A worried man
A macho man
A weak man
Argumentative, sociable, unsociable
A handsome man, a goofy man and
Hard to get to know
Been told I'm…
A great guy
A cool guy
A hot guy
A tough guy

Too serious
A fun guy, a miserable guy
Old-fashioned, new age
Passionate, insightful, pessimistic and
Hard to please.

And been called…
A bastard
A wanker
A joker
Aloof, uncaring, intense, sensitive
Generous
An idiot
Courageous and a coward.

It's no wonder
I sometimes wonder
When I look in a mirror
What other people think of me
Can one really be so complex?

Sorry, I Forgot

I live a long way from
My closest friends and family
So don't see them too often.
We are all now much older and
I'm often moved to wonder
If dementia
Is just around the bend.

Little incidents and signs
Alert me to the possibility.
For example
I forget
To turn off the oven.
My wife forgets to
Pack the chocolates for our Sunday picnic and
We both keep forgetting
To check the oil in the car.
Even my ageing dog sometimes
Doesn't find the treats that I always leave
In the same place.

Then, from afar
A dear friend tells me
She mailed my birthday card
And Christmas greetings but
Long after the events
They haven't arrived.
Were they, perhaps, sent to an address
Of my distant past?

Our good friend Ann
Tells her husband, Boston Bob,
In our company
That he should not smoke, not drink and instead
Buy books of poetry
An odd piece of advice
To a man like Boston Bob
Something I don't believe
Boston could ever contemplate.

So, with all friends and family
Now deep into the autumn of life
And we are constantly informed by experts that
Alzheimers is on the rise
Running amok amongst the ageing population
One feels it necessary to consider
Has anyone yet
Caught it!

Love Her Madly

Several of us in town
Are mad about the doctor
Our doctor
Madly impressed, that is
As she brings almost instant relief
To a sickly condition.
As you first sight her
Intelligent, fresh, natural image and a welcome
With honesty and sincerity
At once you feel
A cure is imminent.
She is not averse to one's preference for
New age remedies or meditation
No lecture or judgement when one owns up
To a lifetime of bad habits.
I receive just a quiet 'You're very lucky
you haven't come a cropper from smoking all those fags'
which, like a statement from a best friend
Makes one think.

Don't we just love her madly
When we're walking out her door.

Now, sadly, she is no longer our doctor
But a specialist in another town
And the only time we get to have
A special consultation
Is when our skin erupts
In dodgy-looking spots.

Facetime

I recently discovered
Facetime
Yet another new you beaut means
Of communication.

Having been brought up with
Landline telephones
Sending letters, birthday and Christmas cards and
The scenic, or cheeky, holiday postcards and
Occasionally sending self-approved recent
Photographs of me
I'm finding it difficult and daunting
Not to mention stressful
To accept into my space
At any time
Unexpected and uninvited persons
And the sometimes unwelcome.

Nowhere to hide
If you're having
A bad hair day.

Escaping Reality

It was great
Those early days
A good time
Exciting, generous, kind
As new things often are.
I loved you
I thought I loved you
All that promise
And looking forward
A long time since
But seems like last year.

I got out
As was the design of my younger life
Always fighting against the tide.
I could foresee
The approaching dull, daily, repetitive
Routine existence
A prison
I would not go to.

I loved you
I thought I loved you.

It's preserved
In my head, imagination, my fantasies
Always young and promising.

And the daily, repetitive grind…
In the end
We all surrender.

Going Back

Took a trip to Christies today
A memory lane visit
Ghosts around every corner
New buildings on every house block.
The main street
Where once there was a grocer store
And a delicatessen
A veg and fruiterer
A fish shop and butcher
A little subterranean bar
That was overrun with drug sellers
A bank for convenience
Which is replaced by
A hole in the wall ATM 20 kilometres away
And the bank building…
Now a tattooist
A hardware store
A delightful restaurant
Now one of five real estate agents
A barber, a newsagent, a health food shop
All now empty.
Further on, the club
My social centre
Acquaintances and conversation friends
Now long departed to where I don't know.

Finally, I cruise past the house on Fenton
Nudging my memory back to
Music-filled, *NagChampa*-spiced, candlelit nights
That didn't wind down
Until the sun came up.

Keeping Secrets

I'm baffled and bemused
By the information and 'secrets'
Some people impart to me
People I barely know
And who certainly barely know me.

My casual pal Bernie
Shows me his betting account and says
If my wife discovered this
She'd probably throw me out.

My acquaintance Janine tells me
Her husband is so wooden and mean.
I've met him once or twice
And found him flexible and kind.

Another mate, Jonathan
Spends a lot of his time
Wanking in front of his laptop.
He didn't say those words, but
One could see in his eyes
And from the content of his searches
That's all you could really surmise.

And the man who's a local legend and
A friend to everyone
States that his wife is a tyrant
His best friend a weakling and
There's no one around he can trust.
But as he tells me these things I wonder
What he says about me and
If I found out
Would I end up distressed and crushed?

These people must know they can trust me
And indeed rest assured that they can.
Their secret thoughts and feelings and actions
Are perfectly kept by me
As I believe only half
Of what I hear and see.

Other Side of the Fence

I know people of
Extreme differing nature
One type that is quiet
Loving, compassionate, considerate and reasonable
The other who is noisy
Cruel, mean, self-centred, nosey and nasty
These people, of course
Make up the world
But in my little world
I know of two such people
The former lives on
The other side of the planet
The latter
On the other side of my garden fence.
I believe
I belong to the former type.

How unfortunate that
In this world of chance, roll the dice and luck
I should be burdened with
The distasteful behaviour, diabolical mouth and
Merciless attitude of a human being
I wish would fall in a hole
And never be seen again.

A Pop Star and Two Politicians

As an exercise
We drew up a shortlist
Of people we'd love to have as
Our next-door neighbour.

Leonard Cohen was an instant
Mutual choice
We've both been under his spell
A warm graceful presence
On a pop music stage
Unique, unrivalled, beautiful
Though sadly now departed.
The next agreed choices were
To my amazement
Politicians.
Bob Brown is a green
Loaded with compassion and commitment
Who gently went about
And brought balance
To the greed and the radical
Another inclusion was
Our favourite current MP
Penny Wong
Who simply exudes intelligence and integrity
Always advocating for justice and equality
Never wavering
No matter who's chucking it at her.

Penny Wong
You're the one
In our dream world
You're our prime minister and
Next-door neighbour.

The Virus 2020

Each morning
Waking up
Into a nightmare.

Never before
Have we wished so much
For everything we had yesterday.

The only freedom now
Is that of the animals and birds
As nature does its thing
To self-regulate.

From **Bindies Only Tickle, 1999**

Repetition

Caught you
Crossing my mind again
And thinking how you led me
Off the crossroads in '68
How you
Found a cure for my busted arm
And how we owed it all to Ron
The great man you wanted me to follow.
Remember
Sitting on the dock of a bay in Essex
Snow-covered Christmas trees and village rooftops
When we were just kids, Kathy
Just kissing.
It stirred me to write my first love poem
Just for you.

I don't know where you might be now
Though I've come across you
Scores of times
And been stirred
Scores of times
To write the same poem
Each time
With different words.

Back Home

Treading familiar old territory
Seeing green green wonderland
Living the way of a traveller
Eating the food of my family
Breathing the air of old homes
Drinking the health of old friends
Sleeping the nights seem so long
Lamenting the time I been gone
Feeling the pain of a song
Laughing happily through a day trip
And wondering where I belong
Waking to the sound of London
And thinking of you and time.

Herbal Remedies

She sits
Very meditative
Her solitude is irresistible.

You don't much care for it
Her long faded black dress
But it hangs on your day.

You don't care also
For the herbal remedies of all ills
Or riding bareback on a beach on Sundays
But it becomes your romance.

The trappings of love.

Seagulls

Seagulls
Laughing sounds
White
Morning sounds
Misty highland morning
Long ago
Misty morning eyes
Missed.

Seagulls
Announce the new day
Beneath the misty morning sky
For the love poet
And you
Seagulls for you
Deep
In the heart of me
Is you.

Diluted

It's scandalous what he does
Your man
Looking cool on the dark velvet lounge
Brushing arms with the girl from Hamburg and
Taking to hand an English–German dictionary.

Your seething blush and rage
Hide in the glowy orange
Of the dimly lit party room.

He wanted to know French and Italian but
Never German
His smile…bigger, brighter than it has been since
You can't remember!

Sorrowful, alone, not sure which way to turn
You sip a little sip
Of a diluted spirit.

Separation

Wake up morning trembling
As I lust for a day
Gone by.
I don't see you there
Sleeping
Waking.
I don't feel your hand
Your hair.
I don't know when
You laugh or
Wipe the tears.

I cash my cheque in
Buy my smokes
And you're a million miles away
Except for
Daydream reality and the pictures.

What a fool to fall
And leave myself these feverish days.

Your town in the early morning
When I'm going home
At night.

From **A Candle For Tomorrow, 2005**

The Sceptic

He sees only what he sees
Through his eyes
And telescope
No confusion for the sceptic
No false horizon from cards and palms and leaves
No expectation from stars and dice and dreams
No lucky stones or magic for the sceptic
No inspiration from anthems, hymns and prayers
No assistance from all the absent gods
No need to fear the words of prophets
With a clear conscience
And knowing nothing lives forever
He wastes no precious time
He knows no other truths, the sceptic
Just the birds who bring his morning
And the love of today.

Dinner For Two

The washing up
I told you not to do
Before you left
The Sunday past
Greets me
Each morning
Each cup of coffee
Each boil of the jug
Each moment…
Caught off guard.

Your lips hover
Around the top of the souvenir glass
Your fingers
Still fondle the cheese slice
Nothing touched
Since you left there
The dinner plates.

Nothing touched
Since you left
And went home.

Looking Back

Looking back
Such a foolish thing to do
The good times get better
The bad times look good.

No chance
Of going back
No way
To have it again
No point
In looking back.

You're Coming Home

As each hour passes
I choke a little.
For ten days
You've been gone
And left me
With a ghost
Left me
With your perfume in my head
Your kiss in my heart
Your voice on the breeze
Left me with your eyes
Looking over me
Your touch
In dreams
Still touching me
Your photo
Haunting, taunting me
Left me with your empty glass
Caressed
By your fingertips
Your absence piercing
My every breath
Your dress longing
To dress you again
And left me with the thought of you
Getting off the train
With all of me waiting
To hold you once again
Left me with the moment I live for
To hold you once again.

Today
You're coming home.

Horses of War

Wandering, one gentle afternoon
Observing horses in a paddock
How attractive they look, graceful.

I peeped inside a church
Not my church
I don't have a church, nor a god
I don't have a god, no religion for me
Never forgotten how cruel he was, god's own messenger.

This church, just a building, though a beautiful building
Spoke a different language
It all means nothing to me
But it's nice to be peaceful, quiet, still.

Inside it invited one to light a candle
Perhaps for a loved departed
I lit a candle for you
I was thinking about you
Not departed
You never came, so you never left.

My burning candle
Burning alone
I shall light another
But for whom?

Almost hypnotised by the peace of the shining flame
A million candles came to light
A candle for every day
For every year
For every century
For every war
Every hunger
Every terror

For every suffering in the name of this church
And that church
For all the people crossing the desert
Crossing the ocean
For the victims of countries, politicians, leaders, societies
The victims of all the gods on earth
For the jungles
The forests
The rivers
For the cow
The chicken
The lamb
Born only to be killed
And a candle for the horses
All the magnificent horses
That men sent to battles
A candle for the horses of war.

From Where Are the Angels, 2015

Celeste

She sits by the window
For ages
She sits
Watching time take the days away
Time…drifting through the day
Washing over everything
Taking it all away.
Discarded summer clothes
And travel maps
Ghosts of friends
Leave short word messages
On the telephone playback
And a great big void.
She was beautiful then
She is beautiful now
All that life
That came and went.
She sits by the window with
Her energy spent
She is beautiful now
With her courage and fear
And a thank you for
The words I give
With a kiss and a single tear.
I leave
With my thoughts to myself
Her weakness in my legs
And on her loneliness
I dwell.
Nothing I could ever have done
Would have made a difference.

One Word

Barely a day has passed
For thirty years
That I haven't thought
Where you are
How you are
About you.

Our fast-lane affair
Booze and sex and cigarettes
Never paused
To see a future
Never slowed down
Until it stopped
And we were never seen again.

Then,
By a fluke
A chance, as is life
I hear you died.
A whole life gone
In a word.

You remain forever
A departing figure through a window
Not wanting to look back
As you left
And remain forever
Someone I always thought I'd see again
Tomorrow.

Not So Tough

Some mornings
When I'm not so tough
I cry
Just like a baby.

Some mornings
Half in life
Half in dreams
I cry as the birds bring me to.

Some mornings
When the sun's still hid
I cry for the love I never gave
For the hellos and goodbyes
For the smile I know
I'll never see again.

Some mornings when I'm not so strong
The tears flow
For mother
Standing in the doorway
And weep
At those times gone
At all the other photographs
Planted eternally
In my mind.

Some mornings
Tears fall for you
Your fathers
Who both
Left too soon.

Some mornings
I just cry
At today's appointments
And when I try to be
A strong and grown-up man
I cry
At my fail mark.

Some mornings I'm awake
Still dreaming
A reality outside the window
Those times gone forever.

And some mornings I know that
These are the days
Sunlight through the trees
My hopes fantasies dreams
Father
Mother
Sister
Brother
Neighbour
Lover
Or friend
Or maybe
Pretend.

But some mornings
When I'm not so tough
I weep
Just like any other baby.

Devastated

It happened when I was seventeen
My girlfriend left me
And later
When I spilt oil on my new shirt
It happened when I missed a concert
By the Stranglers
And when my football team were beaten
In a semifinal
It happened when
My horse lost the Derby
And when
I reached fifty…
No one remembered.

Then…
Something happened…
Something happened
And I finally knew
The true meaning of the word.

Looking For Exits

She came for one night only
Whirling in
Ahead of unforeseen passion
She's looking for the exits
Watch out for the signs.

All through the next day I falter
Around my brittle mind
And write this verse of you:
There are strands of hair on the sofa
Your invisible legs dangling over
Your emotions attached to the curtains, the wall
Your words of unhappiness and ending it all
Your tears stained into the carpet
My tears, layered over them, of little consolation
Your desire's swept up in the morning after
I clutch your wine glass
Still filled with your pain and misadventure.

I walk about this room
Drenched in your sorrow
Wishing I could have set you free.
She's looking for the exits
Watch out for the signs.

Lost For Words

Lying back
In my well worn black banana chair
Time for a little relaxation
Under the peppercorn tree
Sun filtering through
Doves and pigeons do their thing in the gentle cooling breeze
I could believe all the world is
At peace.

Moments later…
A tradies truck rolls up
For business next door
How yer going and happy greetings ensue
Three-way conversations begin…
'It's a fucking lovely day, mate'
'It'll be fucking better when youse get this fucking job done'
'How's the missus, mate?'
'Ah, she's fucking whingeing about the fucking mess around the place'
'They're all the fucking same, mate'
'Yeah, no fucking pleasing them'
On and on it goes
It's friendly enough
But not poetry to my ears
They're all lost for words!

A Mystery (The Sentimental Bloke)

I open the door for her
And treat her to candles
On the restaurant table
I like the mutual
And the sensual
And she responds in kind
I'm a sentimental bloke.

He takes her to the
Second-rate pub diner
Under fluoro lights
Expresses his desire
And speaks…
In second-rate clichés
He's not a sentimental bloke.

I express my concern
For the big wide world
My simple dream
For love and peace
My sorrow
At the removal of trees
To make way
For a new office block and
She responds in kind.

He tells her
Of his previous wife
He has no regrets
That he left it all behind
And they had
Some wonderful times
And he only looks ahead
Does not think about it anymore
And says
'I'm not a sentimental bloke.'

I point out to her…
The beautiful moonlight
Over the bay
How it makes me feel…
Blessed
And in tune
She responds in kind and says
'You're a sentimental bloke.'

He tells her that
It's not his thing
To stroll in the moonlight
Look out across the night
To remember yesterday
To indulge in foreplay.

There's little time to lose
So what will she choose
She's a sentimental woman my lover
My muse.

Then,
In the final act
She…
Takes the road
To his brave new world.

Contrasting Views

Thank you
For the verse you sent me by Kabir
For spiritual uplifting
Though it hasn't brought an end
To my bout of self-pitying.
I don't have
Any feelings or thoughts
Or belief of God
Or a god.
I don't believe anything's pre-planned
Was meant to be
Or is born again.
And I don't believe
In karma.
I have faith only
In nature
Where everything is equal
And a future dependent on
Evolution, chance and luck.
In nature
Things happen…
Just because they do.
There's no intent to kill
Unless for survival
No intent to hurt
No intent to upset.

There is life
Followed by death
Be it an insect
Animal
Human being
Or planet.
I believe this is the truth
And inevitable.
One life
One death.

Only WE believe.
Everything else knows and senses
And accepts.
Nature and chance
Gave me life
Just as it will end it.
And everyday
Is like a new life.
My spirit dances in it.
Just a pity being laden with
The human condition
And worrying about things
Instead of accepting them.
As my dog does.
The End.
Amen.

Gardening

Digging here digging there
So much of my time in thought.
I want to do the garden
Not fight myself to a clear mind
Or be somewhere I can't be.
My choices are made
So what have I learnt…
I'm elevated beyond regret
Smarter than those that would
Deceive me.
I prefer simple
To sophisticated
Silence
Over clatter.
I love kindness, honesty,
TRUTH.

There's a screen put up
What is this!
What's going on…
Behind my back
Right in front of my eyes?

On the Grass

Today…what a waste of time
A waste of a short day
Waiting
Wasting
Longing
My new doctor was very attentive
Though just another 50-50 chance.

The waiting room
I do a lot of thinking…waiting
On reflection…more wasted time
And longing
I long to sprawl out on the grass
On the grass
Not on the phone
Not on a cruise
Not on a drinking jaunt
Not on a promise
Just a simple bed of grass
And talk
For hours
With a long-time trusted friend.

Prime Cuts

Yesterday
Going about their usual business
The day spent breathing the sweet
Spring-filled air
Of freedom
And life
Contented
Frolicking
And munching their way
Through the day
As it all should be.
The wonderful sight
Of contentment
Drifting easy
Across the plains.

Today
In the prime of their lives
They are in a grim place
Breathing the air of death.
They are those about to die
For prime cuts.

The Priest Hood

Quiet dark room
Holy Holy
Evil
Nowhere is safe
The father
The torturer
No one to trust.

Thirty years on
The whole world
A quiet dark room
Nowhere is safe
No one to trust.

Quiet dark room
A hood over a lifetime.

From **Night Café & other poems, 2016**

Everything Becomes Nothing

As he comforted his
Aged, dying friend
A conversation was struck
The last meaningful one
Greg would have with Richard.
It's all rather stupid.
What is, Richard?
Life, he replied.
There doesn't seem any point
All the stuff I've treasured
And protected
And insured
All the people I've met
And tried to possess
All the money I've made
All the worry, anxiety and stress.
Now I've got this
My only comfort, my bed
In a strange, unfamiliar place
And cling to the consolation
Of a few visits
By trusted friends
Like yourself.
Everything becomes nothing.
Don't waste time, Greg
Life is today, now, this minute
For you
And for me
Don't worry about your things
They're just on loan.

I don't have
A god
To go to
I don't wake up any more and think
What will I do next
In my life
I don't know
Why I read all those books
About life
About why we're here
And how to be happy
And how to be successful
Always searching for reasons
And answers
Instead of just living it.
And
I don't even have
A dying wish.

Forgiven

You say you're sorry
For our demise
Blame yourself
For the deceit and lies
But it's balanced it's equal
We're two different people
We just ran out of luck
Ran out of time
To be who you are
And feel what you feel
Is not bad or wrong
Not a sin or a crime

I forgive you my love for
Cheating on me
I don't call it cheating
Just branching out, being free

I forgive you for believing
You've wasted my time
Time is here for us
To use up

I forgive you for
Misunderstanding me
We are all unique
All separate, all a mystery

I forgive you for walking
When we should have been running
We missed our chance
But there's always another train coming

I forgive you for putting
Your trust in God
I advised he may be absent
And he never came
When you said he would

I forgive you for
Voting conservative
You know very little of
The alternative

And I forgive you for
Being angry with me
It wasn't enough to not give a stuff
There was a stand to take
You wanted to sit down
I had to stand up

In the end it came out
As it always does
You had to sit down
I wanted to stand up.

In My Dreams

Some things
In this life
Are destined to never be.

The most beautiful
The most bewitching
The most appealing
The most desirable
The most heart-throbbing woman
I ever met
Was a lesbian.

Coincidence

Some people
Have terrible lives
Bad deals
Bad luck
No breaks
No love.

Forget your god, your prayers
There may be
A coincidence
That will give you claim
To your belief
A miracle, a cure, a resolution
But coincidence
Like a storm
Just happens
Every now and again.

Funeral Atrocity

The guests gather
At the after event party
Mostly dressed in jeans, T-shirts
Training suits, running shoes
For a casual afternoon of
Drinking, joking
Catch up, smoking.
The dead man was
A gentleman
Gentle
Generous
Sober
He had an inheritance
Enjoyed to shout the bar
It disguised a loner.
I
As usual
Was the observer
Often perceived too
As a loner.
The hilarity was rank
The jokes vulgar
The respect non-existent.
Again
As usual
I try to see the good in all.
Everybody wants fun, a good time, a laugh.

Maybe
It was relief
That the dead gentleman
Was dead
And not them.

Record Collection

It's accompanied me
For more than fifty years
Growing in size
From a few 45s
Growing in status and taste
My only prized possession
Treasured all my life
Priceless to me
My diary, my history.

There are red-wine-splattered album covers
Of Dylan, Bowie and Cream
Smoke-coated single sleeves of
Love, Kinks, the Music Machine
Loads of Beatles, Queen and Byrds
There's rock and folk, jazz and punk
New Wave, classical
And some junk
Pink Floyd, Donovan, Horslips and Who
Gorecki, Velvet Underground and
Music From the World series 2.

It is a
Spiritual existence
That has lived with me
In countless homes
Travelled across
Continents and countries
In a crate through customs
In cartons on a trailer across cities.

Almost every individual disc
Has its own special unique
Meaning, memory
Inducing emotional responses
Bringing back bits of time
That make me sigh
Remember, cry
Nostalgic
Thoughtful
Grateful.
Handled with care
Some are ragged
Around the edges
Not unlike myself
We're both of us vintage
I search for one
An LP all-time favourite of mine
Been thinking for days
I've got to hear it again
I ease it from the stack
And play a track
'Dream Within A Dream'
What does it mean?
It's Spirit, 1969
My summer of love
A beautiful time.

Returning the record
To its age-worn cover
I spot a hair in its fold
Still brown, but old
Astonished
Overcome
Could it be yours!
Or mine
From 1969?

Remembering Grandad

I remember grandad
One lasting image
From 1961 I think
Because I recall hearing
'Walking Back To Happiness'
By Helen Shapiro on the wireless
And my dad telling his dad
I love this song.

Grandad just sat there
Only ever a hint
Of a smile
I believe he was about sixty
But my image has him looking
More like eighty
Even older.
He was damaged
By two wars
In 1916 as a soldier
In the early 40s as
A wounded civilian
Caught up in the bombing of London.

He'd had it with the Germans
Two generations had
Totally destroyed his life.
Hitler was the most
Blasphemous word he knew.

He wouldn't talk about it
Just grunt some hatred.
He looked pathetic.
Each part of him
Was injured
Irrevocably.

I was young
Twelve
And didn't comprehend all of this
I thought only that
He was old
And crippled.
There were medals
Casually placed
On a sideboard.
From a recollection
Of their mention
He didn't much care for them.
Today
Men
With that kind of history
Though not nearly as severe
Are called heroes
Treated as heroes
Regarded as heroes.

They weren't called heroes then
There was no
Special treatment for them
No one came calling
To his run-down, falling down
Two-up two-down house
Barely patched up since an encounter with a bomb
Some fifteen to twenty years earlier.
No one came calling
To offer support, aid.

He didn't look like a hero
To me, at twelve
And he certainly
Never thought himself one
And why would he?
Grandad wasn't a hero
Wasn't treated as one
Wasn't regarded as one
He wasn't an illustrious warrior
Never performed heroic achievements.

Remembering grandad, I recall
A frail, humble, gentle man
Full of misery
Who displayed kindness and generosity
Towards my brother and me
With sixpence and a handful of sweets
On each occasion we saw him.

He was unlucky
To have been born in 1900 England.
He had no choice
He was sent to do his duty
With millions of others
To do what he could, to take his chances
Then left to deal
With the consequences.

He had a dreadful life
Which ended shortly
After this lasting-image visit.

You Make Loving Fun

Nature
I'm in love with you
You never disappoint
Never let me down
All your moods
Your calm your rage
I accept
You're the complete guide
That brings me through each day
The sun
Big eye in the sky
The tree
Strong and still
Insects
Busy and bold
The birds
Fluttering and vibrant
I don't know the species
It doesn't matter
The birdwatcher studies them
For information, facts
To catalogue, categorise
It's admirable
I see their behaviour
To adjust my mood
Tickle my fancy
Enhance my wonder

Nature
You're my very breath
The air the rain the sun
All the beautiful creatures
You
Make loving fun.

From **A Long Way From Essex, 2019**

Seven Shades of Grey

Many good old pals
Are facing the ultima
We're all equal
As each of us find out.

Pierre says bugger it all
Just gonna do what I like to do
Sally takes a different view, one day at a time
One day crying, the next with a smile
Harold is an optimist
Fearing the worst but planning ahead
Terry is a mystery
Still has his cigarettes between
Chemotherapy
Johno is a total wreck
Keeps crashing down, hitting the deck
Poor old Robbie is concerned only about looks
He's abandoned his philosophy, music and books
And jolly old Kim
Thinks it'll all work out
Has a drink and a laugh
Nothing ever bothers him.
While I
With the same total years behind
Count my blessings
Keep a good heart
And consider my next gamble.

Coffee Card

There's an elderly guy
I pass most mornings
Sitting at the edge of an outdoor area
Of a local café
His motorised wheelchair stationed nearby.
He's been there for months
Every day
Dressed in raggedy clothes
Looks like a war veteran
A Vietnam vet perhaps
And poverty-stricken
Though a bit presumptuous to
Judge by appearance.

Always alone
I feel inclined to drop him my change
Or even a crisp fifty-dollar note.
He gestures in a very friendly manner
Towards me, and my dog
And watches intently if I leave my dog tied to a post
Whilst I pop to the shop next door
And delights upon seeing me return
My dog wagging her tail, ecstatic to see me again
He appears to cherish the reunion
Of me and my dog.

I strike up a brief Good Morning conversation with him
'Enjoying your coffee?'
He nods, with a
Beaming, toothless smile
I say 'Do you have a coffee card?'
He shakes his head
Not knowing what the hell I'm talking about.

I explain, 'Six coffees and the next one's free'
Five bucks a week he could save
Every other person there, cashed-up
Present theirs for a stamp or a freebie
And it bothers me that
None of the three staff or manager
Concerned so with their busyness
Has ever thought
To give him
A coffee card.

If Not For You

I have an Aboriginal friend
Mixed race Australian/European
An activist, campaigner for rights
And I detect
The bitterness
That stems
From the invasion.
I share her view.

Conscious of not wanting to appear
To play down
The enormous consequence
Of the big issue
I,
Being me,
True to nature
Cherish life
Always looking for a positive
Suggested that
Just for a moment
Look at the
Smaller picture
Personally
If not for the invasion
Jessie
You would not have
Been born
And we wouldn't know each other.

It makes nothing right and,
Makes nothing wrong.
This is
As it is.

Now He's Gone

You kept on saying
He drives me mad
I wish he'd go out
That'll make me glad
One of his long boating trips or
Spend more time at
The mens shed
Go overseas with all his pals
And I could see you thinking
Maybe even find a new romance
He's not the man I married
He used to make me laugh.

Forty-something years
You've been together
Shared your living, your love
Your eating
Your dancing
Your sleeping
Your sorrow and grief.

I said, half in jest
Be careful
What you're wishing for, Janice
Everything comes and
Everything goes.

Now
You're inconsolable
He had a pain
You thought would go away
He had a pain
You'd never planned for
It brought him down
And now he's gone.

Is this what you wanted, all along
You sit at home
Can't play his favourite song
All the time feeling you have
Nowhere to belong.

You never thought
What it would be like
Now that he's gone.

Alone Again Or

Becoming seventy
It's mind-boggling
'Having a party, Doug?'
I think not
Just quietly see it through
Spend the time with you.

I never thought I'd reach
This milestone
As a young hippy
We never wanted to be that old generation
Whom mostly despised us
And whom we
Wanted to replace
With a new agenda
Of love and flowers and peace.

Now,
We've all become our parents, our grandparents
Dispersed
Throughout the world
Alone with the dreams
The flowers growing today
Being readied for our graves.
Many cling to some faith and
Look forward to
Uniting with their god
So as to never
Be
Alone.

I don't have such delusions or expectations
We are all alone
From birth
We have attachments
And detachments
Cling to this person, or that person
And let go
We cling to family, wealth and books
And let go
To things and ideals
To health and looks
And let go
We cling to life itself
Then let go.

The only time
We're not alone
Is when
We're in
The womb.

Averages

My mate Will is
An averages man
The law of averages
He applies it to everything
He tells me,
'We live for about
Thirty thousand days.'
Sounds a lot different
To eighty years
One moment sounding like
Forever
Until one does the sums
At sixty-eight
I've already had twenty-five thousand!
And days pass
Very quickly.

He bombards me with
Statistics and projections
How certain it is that
Because THIS occurs
THAT will follow, and so on.
He says it's balance.

Will is an average kind of man
Lives an average life
In an average kind of place
A gated village
For the over sixty fives.
He says:
'No one there realises
The life they have left
Is just days
They do nothing with them
Sit around
Waiting for that final day
They see life
Looking from behind their see through curtains'
Which he observes
Blowing in the breath.

He says,
'It all averages out
So much per cent of this
So much per cent of that
The average man
Has his share
Of good days and
Bad days
He'll have
So many wins
So many losses
You can't defy it
Can't deny it.'

I enjoy discussing philosophy with my mates.

This is
The most scintillatingly fascinating
Boring and
A tad disturbing
Piece of information
Anyone has ever given me.
Fatalistic, though consoling
Confronting, though thought provoking
Encouraging and inevitable
Sobering.

Will says,
'If today's a shit of a day
Don't dwell on it
The averages say a good day is due.

Look back on your life
And see how the good
Followed bad
And the bad followed good.
Let the averages
Have their way
And don't resist.'

I went home
And thought about it.
Of course, he's right.
At seventy-seven
Will's got a thousand days left.

A Day After Dying

So,
What the fuck was that all about!
Ducking and diving
Deceiving and lying
Believing, denying
Laughing and crying
All the heartache
The pain
The losses, the gains
It all came and went
Like an express train.

Where to now?
There's nothing around
Not a sky, not a ground
Not even a sound.

So, what on earth was that all about
Everything's gone
It's come to the end
Nothing here to protect
Nothing left to defend
It's over, it's out
The end of the bout.

Baiting and Waiting

Sometimes I think about
The carnage I cause
To the parallel
Miniature
World
And the power
We have over it.

I place the baits
Amongst the often crumbs strewn area
Around the bread bin.
I occasionally observe
As the industrious, loyal to their queen, ants
Dutifully take the offering
Return to camp
And thus wipe out
The whole colony.

I'm never quite sure I should feel
Clever and self satisfied
That I've fixed a problem.

Would I do this
Were it to be reported on the news
With graphic zoomed in pictures
Of the suffering
Or
Maybe
Think of a way
We could live in this world together.

The Lonely Sun

It stands supreme
The omnipotent presence
In the sky.

The sun is the visible god
It giveth life
It taketh life
Nothing is eternal
No need to seek an invisible power
It's there for you
Every day
The sun will have
The final say.

The sun is the light, the power
The sun is unapproachable
The veil around us
Protects from its fury
We destroy it…and only then
Will the sun react in anger.

It's there for you
Every day
All-powerful
With the final say.

www.ingramcontent.com/pod-product-compliance
Lightning Source LLC
Chambersburg PA
CBHW070905080526
44589CB00013B/1192